ALL the FISH in the WORLD

David Opie

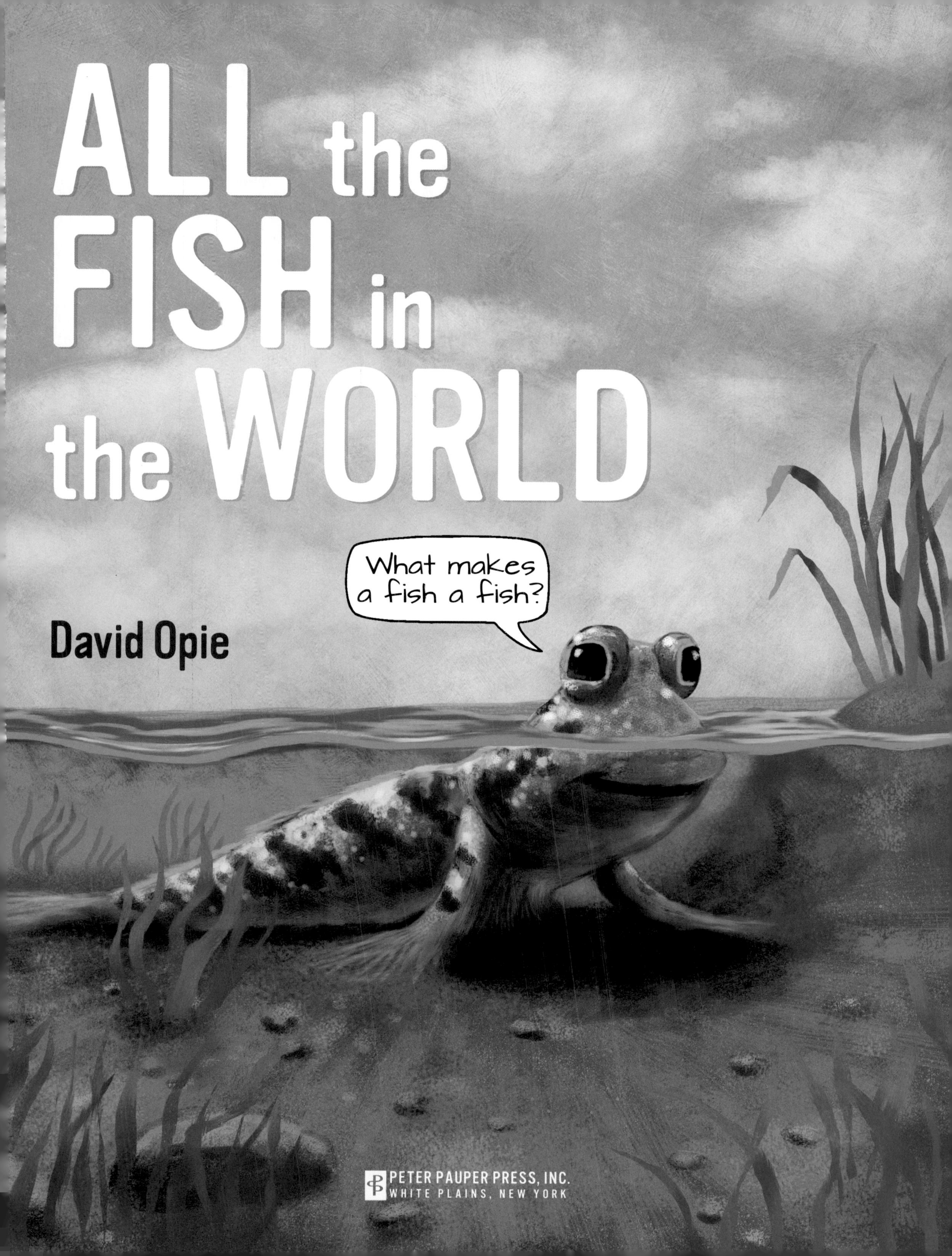

PETER PAUPER PRESS, INC.
WHITE PLAINS, NEW YORK

Dedicated to my mom.
Thanks for a lifetime of love, encouragement, and support.

Text and illustrations copyright © 2021 by David Opie
All rights reserved. No part of this book may be used or reproduced
in any manner whatsoever without written permission from the publisher.
First edition 2021

Published by Peter Pauper Press, Inc.
202 Mamaroneck Avenue
White Plains, New York 10601 USA

Library of Congress Cataloging-in-Publication Data

Names: Opie, David, author, illustrator.
Title: All the fish in the world / David Opie.
Description: First edition. | White Plains, New York : Peter Pauper Press, Inc.,2021.
| Audience: Ages 3 to 8 | Audience: Grades K-1 | Summary:
"What makes a fish a fish? Trout thinks he knows the answer.
"That's easy! Fish have fins, gills, scales, are shaped like me, and live
underwater." "Not so fast," answers Mudskipper. "What about a clingfish?
They don't have any scales. Or a hagfish? They don't have any fins. Or
what about me? I live in and out of the water!" As Trout and Mudskipper
explore below and above the world's waters, they are introduced to a
multitude of fish in various shapes, colors, and sizes, forcing Trout to
rethink about his notion of what a fish is. Maybe there is a vast watery
world of unimagined possibilities (like a walking fish, or a fish with a
transparent head!). And maybe, just maybe, there's not just one way to
be a fish-but many, many ways!"-- Provided by publisher.
Identifiers: LCCN 2020042648 | ISBN 9781441335784 (hardcover)
Subjects: LCSH: Fishes--Juvenile literature.
Classification: LCC QL617.2 .O65 2021 | DDC 597--dc23
LC record available at https://lccn.loc.gov/2020042648

ISBN 978-1-4413-3578-4
Manufactured for Peter Pauper Press, Inc.
Printed in China

7 6 5 4 3 2 1

Visit us at www.peterpauper.com

"What makes a fish a fish?"
asked Mudskipper.

"That's easy," answered Trout.
"Fish are like me!
They have scales,
pairs of fins, and backbones.
Fish live underwater,
are cold-blooded,
and breathe through gills."

"Not so fast," said Mudskipper.
"What about me?"

Over 33,000 species of fish live in the world.
Many have fins, scales, gills,
wedge-shaped heads, and tapered tails
perfectly shaped for slicing through water.

"See," said Trout. "Just like me!"

But there is a multitude of fish
in various shapes, colors, and sizes,
that move, breathe, and mate
in different ways.

Some fish may be shaped like
dinner plates, balloons, ribbons,
or even leafy plants
to blend into their surroundings.

The largest fish, the whale shark,
can be longer than a school bus,
while one of the smallest, the stout floater,
grows only as long as the word "fish" on this page.

"Whoa, I didn't know there were fish this big!" said Trout.

There are so many brightly-hued fish
streaking through oceans, lakes, and streams,
like the brilliant royal blue tang, with a flash of yellow,
or the royal gramma, with its purple face
and rich golden tail.
There's the deep red of the spawning sockeye salmon,
and the large splotches of orange
on the koi's back, and every shade of green and gray,
and flickers of silver.

Wild patterns spatter all over some fish.
False eyes stare back,
and bars and spots and stripes,
can break up the fish's shape,
and confuse animals searching for a meal
among the tangle of weeds and stones and reefs.

"Okay, so fish can come in all types of shapes, sizes, and colors, but all fish have to have scales, right?"

"Not exactly."

Almost all fish are covered in scales,
those little overlapping discs,
like chain mail protecting a knight.
The sturgeon and armored catfish have thick, bony plates,
and sharks have scales like rough, overlapping little teeth.
But hagfish, clingfish, and some eels
have no scales at all.

"Well, one thing I know for sure is that all fish definitely have fins."

"Hmmm . . .
I wouldn't be so sure."

Almost all fish have paired fins,
those wings that push them through the water,
steer them around rocks and coral,
and hide them among the grasses.
Fins take many forms,
depending on their uses.
But the hagfish has no true fin at all.
Instead it has only a flattened tail
to sweep it forward
as it wiggles along the ocean floor.

There is a fascinating group of fish whose skeletons are not made of bones, but are made of a flexible, rubber-like tissue called cartilage. (Humans have cartilage, too—in places like the tips of their noses where it's stiff but bendy.)
This boneless group of fish includes sharks, skates, chimaeras, and rays.

"Trout, where did you go?" said Mudskipper.

Some fish live and dive in the deep, dark depths of the ocean,
so far down that the sun's rays can't reach them.
Some of these deep-sea fish create their own light:
they have glowing parts
like fireflies in a summer field.
And some of those fish,
swimming far below the waterline,
have spooky names, like sabertooth, daggertooth,
fangtooth, blobfish, viperfish, devil ray, and goblin shark.

"That's too far down for me."

"Me too."

Some fish build beds
for attracting a mate,
and for laying eggs.
The cichlid constructs a mound like a castle.
A bluehead chub piles up stones to make a nest.
The white-spotted pufferfish makes a large patterned circle.
A triggerfish scoops out a bowl in the sand,
while the stickleback weaves together a grass nest,
and betta fish will blow a raft of bubbles.

Most fish lay eggs,
sometimes thousands at a time.
Some fish keep the eggs inside their bodies
until they hatch, and the baby fish swim out.
Many sharks give birth to live babies called pups,
and other types of sharks, rays, and skates
hang their eggs onto seagrass and kelp,
or hide their egg cases on the sea floor
in rocky crevices and among plants
where they remain hidden
until they hatch.

Fish have developed many ways
to sense the world around them.
The catfish has whiskers
to feel its way around the murky bottom.
A few fish can sense when something interrupts
the electric field they create around their bodies.
And some fish, like sharks and piranhas,
have a very strong sense of smell.
The barreleye fish swivels its eyes
from deep inside its transparent head.
A flounder is born with eyes
on both sides of its head, but then, as it grows,
one eye moves over to join
the other so they're both looking up.

"My eyes see better
in air than in water,"
said Mudskipper.

"You can
see in air?"

Almost all fish swim to get around,
flapping their fins
as they shimmy through the water.
But some can move in other ways.
The climbing perch and snakehead fish
can scoot short distances on land!
The flying fish, when being chased,
can launch out of the water,
stretch out its long, wing-like fins,
and glide to safety.
The frogfish, batfish, and spotted handfish,
can pull themselves along on their fins,
taking a stroll along the ocean floor.

"Just wait till you see what
I can do," said Mudskipper.

Most fish live and breathe underwater.
They pull water, and the oxygen in it,
into their mouths, and over their gills,
collecting the oxygen
that all animals need to survive.
But a few fish,
like the knifefish, the lungfish, the arapaima, and the snakehead
can gulp air from above the waterline.

And then there's the amazing mudskipper,
who lives along the shoreline and
can take in a mouthful of water
and store it in its gill chambers,
much like a chipmunk stores food in its cheeks.
Then, using its front fins as legs,
the mudskipper can crawl, almost skipping,
through the mud and onto land,
where it can stay for a couple days,
before it heads back into the water
with the other fish.

"Pretty impressive, huh?"
said Mudskipper.

"Wow, I never knew a fish
could do all that."

"Fish can do all sorts of amazing things," said Mudskipper. "Whether they have fins, scales, bones, gills, live above or below water, fish are fascinating creatures. There's never just one way to be a fish."

"You're right," said Trout. "There's thousands of ways!"

Over 33,000 ways, to be a little more precise.

A Note from the Author

Life on our home planet originated in water, and the first fish developed about 530 million years ago, long before birds and mammals. Biologists estimate that there are over 33,000 species of fish, while there are about 10,000 species of birds, and just over 5,000 kinds of mammals. Birds and mammals (including us humans) evolved from ancient fish.

Steelhead trout

In this book, Mudskipper asks what makes a fish a fish, and Trout finds out that answering that question can be complicated. Part of the issue is that "fish" is not really a technical term; it is merely a convenient way to refer to a large group of diverse animals. When we think about "fish," we usually picture something like a trout: streamlined shape, paired fins, covered in scales, living in water, breathing through gills, having a spinal column and skeleton, and unable to regulate its body temperature (which is an ability that we mammals have).

Mangrove rivulus

As I've written in this book, there are exceptions to every one of those assumptions I've listed above: Fish come in many different shapes, and not all are streamlined. Hagfish have only a flattened area of the tail, and no paired fins. Some eels have no scales, and the armored catfish and sturgeon are clad in bony plates (called "scutes") instead of scales. And what about gills? Australian lungfish gulp air above the waterline and absorb oxygen into their lungs, hence their name. Several other fish, like the mudskipper, American and European eels, and the mangrove rivulus, can absorb oxygen directly through their damp skin. As far as being water-bound, mudskippers can spend a majority of their lifetimes outside of the water (as long as they're in a damp environment), and African lungfish can wait out droughts by burying themselves in a mucus-lined burrow and breathing air into their lungs through a small hole.

Hagfish are the exception to having a skeleton. Although they do have partial skulls, their bodies are supported by a structure made of cartilage called a notochord, and they have no actual spinal column.

Although fish can generally be considered cold-blooded (their bodies are the same temperature as their surroundings), some sharks can raise their body temperatures significantly through physical exertion, and the opah, or moonfish, is considered a true warm-blooded fish.

Hagfish

So, what can we say about *all* fish? Well, *all* fish have a brain in a protective case, a head region with sensory organs, and they have blood flowing through their bodies. That doesn't really narrow it down much, does it? What we can say about *all* fish though is that they are members of a dynamic and diverse group of creatures that hold a wealth of information about our past, present, and future.

And unfortunately, fish are in danger throughout the world, due mainly to overfishing, loss of habitat, and climate change. The International Union for the Conservation of Nature (IUCN), the largest global organization that helps endangered species, estimates that 5 percent of all fish species—and a quarter of all sharks and rays—are endangered. Fish are vital to our ecosystem, and we need to protect them. To find more information and learn how you can help, please go to www.iucn.org.

I hope this book serves as an introduction to the strange and wonderful world of fish, and demonstrates what a wide range of creatures exist in the fish family. I also hope that you will be inspired to learn more about them and will do what you can to help preserve fish of all shapes, sizes, and colors.

Cover

1. Sailfin flying fish
2. Barred mudskipper
3. Atlantic bluefin tuna
4. John Dory
5. Blacktip reef shark
6. Fairy wrasse
7. Soldierfish
8. Yellow wrasse
9. Royal blue tang
10. Striped burrfish
11. Forceps butterflyfish
12. Lyretail anthias
13. Seahorse
14. Steelhead trout
15. Cuban hogfish
16. Yellow tang
17. Porcupinefish

18. Common hatchetfish (F)
19. Lionfish
20. Longhorn cowfish
21. Panther grouper
22. Goliath grouper
23. Tarpon
24. Red gurnard
25. Clownfish

26. Lineatus fairy wrasse
27. Royal gramma
28. Moorish idol
29. Herring
30. Royal angelfish
31. Garibaldi
32. Sand tiger shark
33. Mandarin dragonet

34. Mahi-mahi
35. Lookdown
36. Flame angelfish
37. Yellow pigeon checkerboard discus (A)
38. Great barracuda
39. French angelfish
40. Old wife

41. Pennantfish
42. Manta ray
43. John Dory
44. Picasso triggerfish
45. Red melon discus (A)
46. Weedy seadragon
47. Lanternfish
48. Atlantic silver hatchetfish

49. Humpback anglerfish
50. Fangtooth
51. Purple tang
52. Yellow boxfish
53. Oarfish
54. Four stripe damselfish
55. Ornate butterflyfish
56. Orange-banded pipefish

Page 1   Barred mudskipper

Pages 2-3 (from left) Steelhead trout, barred mudskipper

Pages 4-5

1. Pacific albacore tuna
2. Atlantic menhaden
3. Sea bass
4. Salmon
5. Barred mudskipper
6. Steelhead trout
7. Atlantic cod
8. Bluefish
9. Striped bass
10. Sea bass
11. Atlantic menhaden
12. Herring
13. Hickory shad
14. Atlantic cod
15. Atlantic mackerel
16. Tarpon
17. Branzino
18. Sea bass
19. Bluefin tuna
20. Sardine

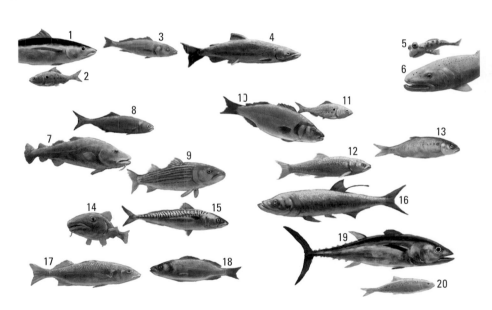

Fish are not necessarily to scale. Some fish in the background are not identified.
Freshwater fish are indicated with (F) after their name. All other fish live in saltwater.
Fish labeled (A), for "Aquarium," have been specially bred by aquarium keepers for their beautiful colors, and look different from wild fish of their species.

Australian lungfish

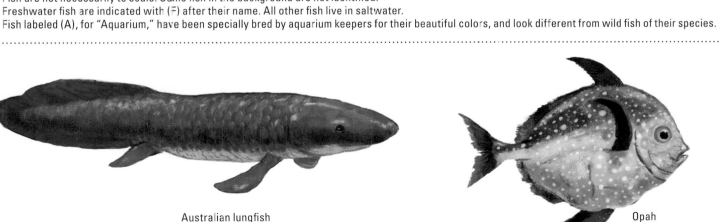

Opah

Pages 6-7

1. Steelhead trout
2. Barred mudskipper
3. Great barracuda
4. Striped burrfish
5. John Dory
6. Alligator gar (F)
7. Porcupinefish
8. Goliath grouper
9. Longhorn cowfish
10. Needlefish
11. Lionfish
12. Ocean sunfish
13. Northern pipefish
14. Stingray
15. Common hatchetfish (F)
16. Leafy seadragon
17. Foxface rabbitfish
18. Purple tang
19. Seahorse

20. Green moray eel
21. Asian sheepshead wrasse
22. Winter flounder
23. Hairy frogfish
24. Spotted garden eels

Pages 8-9

1. Whale shark
2. Steelhead trout
3. Mudskipper

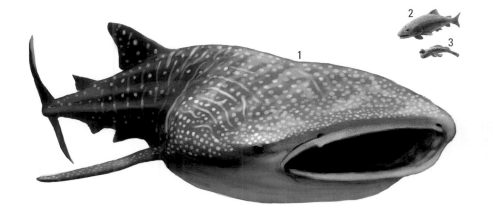

Pages 10-11

1. Koi (F) (A)
2. Goldfish (F) (A)
3. Sockeye salmon
4. Barred mudskipper
5. Steelhead trout
6. Filefish
7. High-hat
8. Fairy wrasse
9. Betta (F) (A)
10. Regal angelfish
11. Garibaldi
12. Yellow pigeon checkerboard discus (A)
13. Four-eyed butterflyfish
14. Yellow tang
15. Red melon discus (A)
16. Panther grouper

17. Yellow wrasse
18. Ornate butterflyfish
19. Emperor angelfish
20. Striped beakfish
21. Forceps butterflyfish
22. Royal gramma
23. Royal blue tang
24. Clownfish
25. Clown triggerfish
26. Banded pipefish
27. Mandarin dragonet

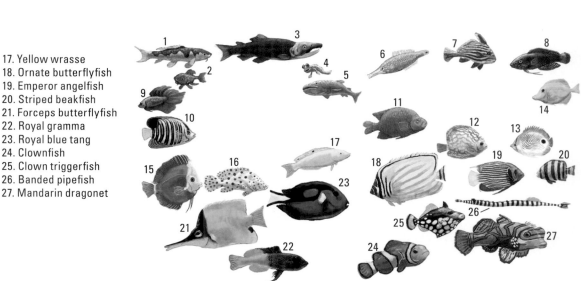

Fish are not necessarily to scale.
Some fish in the background are not identified.
Freshwater fish are indicated with (F) after their name. All other fish live in saltwater.
Fish labeled (A), for "Aquarium," have been specially bred by aquarium keepers for their beautiful colors, and look different from wild fish of their species.

Pages 12-13

1. Steelhead trout
2. Mudskipper
3. Common carp (F)
4. Asian arowana (F)
5. Coelacanth
6. Armored catfish
7. Hagfish
8. American eel
9. Clingfish
10. Sturgeon
11. Rudd
12. Herring
13. Sand tiger shark
14. Atlantic tarpon

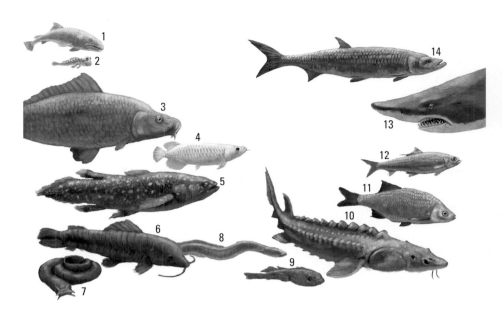

Pages 14-15

1. Great white shark
2. Pennantfish
3. Gulf darter (F)
4. Arctic grayling (F)
5. Steelhead trout
6. Barred mudskipper
7. Sailfish
8. Pacific fanfish
9. Bluegill (F)
10. Peacock cichlid (F) (A)
11. Tripodfish
12. Hagfish
13. Lookdown
14. Red gurnard
15. Sailfin molly (F) (A)
16. Yellow cobra guppy (F) (A)
17. Betta (F) (A)
18. Freshwater angelfish (F)

Pages 16-17

1. Hammerhead shark
2. Great white shark
3. Manta ray
4. Barred mudskipper
5. Silky shark
6. Sawfish
7. Manta ray
8. Thresher shark
9. Blacktip reef shark
10. Shortfin mako shark
11. Steelhead trout
12. Skate
13. Nurse shark
14. Spotted ratfish (a "chimaera,"
     pronounced KY-MEER-UH)

Fish are not necessarily to scale.
Some fish in the background are not identified.
Freshwater fish are indicated with (F) after their name. All other fish live in saltwater.
Fish labeled (A), for "Aquarium," have been specially bred by aquarium keepers for their beautiful colors, and look different from wild fish of their species.

Pages 18-19

1. Barred mudskipper
2. Steelhead trout
3. Daggertooth
4. Giant devil ray
5. Sabertooth
6. Pelican eel
7. Fangtooth
8. Lanternfish
9. Goblin shark
10. Atlantic silver hatchetfish
11. Humpback anglerfish
12. Lanternfish
13. Atlantic bigeye tuna
14. Oarfish
15. Frilled shark
16. Telescopefish
17. Viperfish
18. Stoplight loosejaw
19. Blobfish

Pages 20-21

1. Steelhead trout
2. Barred mudskipper
3. White-spotted pufferfish
4. Cichlid (F)
5. Bluehead chub (F)
6. Betta (F) (A)
7. Dogfish egg case, sometimes referred
   to as a "mermaid's purse"
8. Port Jackson shark egg case
9. Titan triggerfish
10. European bullhead (F)
11. Ninespine stickleback (F)

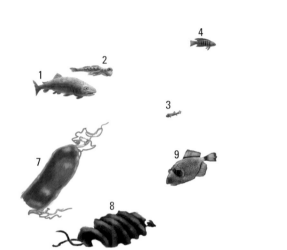

Pages 22-23

1. Catfish (F)
2. Elephantnose fish (F)
3. Red-bellied piranha (F)
4. Pyjama shark
5. Black ghost knifefish (F)
6. Barred mudskipper
7. Steelhead trout
8. Marbled electric ray
9. Blacktip reef shark
10. Electric eel (F)
11. Winter flounder
12. Barreleye

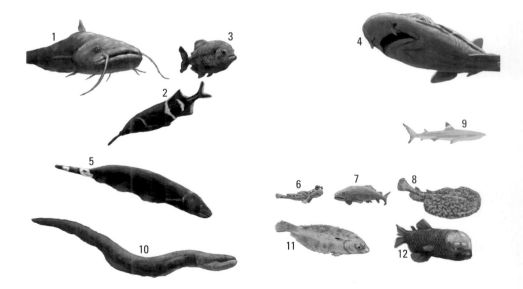

Fish are not necessarily to scale.
Some fish in the background are not identified.
Freshwater fish are indicated with (F) after their name. All other fish live in saltwater.
Fish labeled (A), for "Aquarium," have been specially bred by aquarium keepers for their beautiful colors, and look different from wild fish of their species.

Pages 24-25

1. Sailfin flying fish
2. Barred mudskipper
3. Climbing perch (F)
4. Mahi-mahi
5. Giant frogfish
6. Steelhead trout
7. Painted frogfish
8. Shortnose batfish
9. Spotted handfish

Pages 26-27

1. Arapaima gigas (F)
2. Northern snakehead (F)
3. Clown knifefish (F)
4. African lungfish (F)
5. Barred mudskipper
6. Steelhead trout

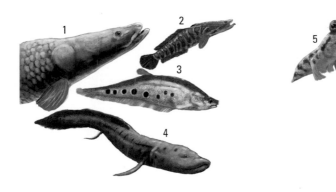

Pages 28-29

1. Map puffer
2. Bluefin tuna
3. Spotted scat
4. Picasso triggerfish
5. Goliath grouper
6. French angelfish
7. Porcupinefish
8. Soldierfish
9. Longhorn cowfish
10. Flame angelfish
11. Moorish idol
12. Weedy seadragon
13. Leopard shark
14. Manta ray
15. Skate
16. Common seahorse
17. Forceps butterflyfish
18. Splendid garden eels
19. Royal gramma
20. Barred mudskipper

21. Steelhead trout
22. Honeycomb moray eel
23. Humpback anglerfish
24. Clownfish
25. Tub gurnard
26. Orange-banded pipefish
27. Summer flounder

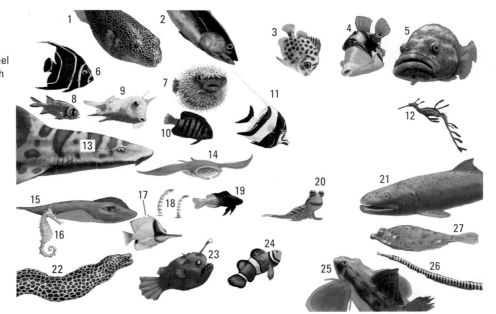

Fish are not necessarily to scale.
Some fish in the background are not identified.
Freshwater fish are indicated with "(F)" after their name. All other fish live in saltwater.

About the Main Characters

Mudskipper

There are over 30 species of mudskippers, found in the Indo-Pacific and coastal Africa. Their most interesting feature is that their front fins are connected to muscles that act more like legs. They can also gulp a huge mouthful of water and fill up their gill chambers, allowing them to get oxygen from the ingested water while they crawl around on land. Their large, bulgy eyes are better adapted to seeing above, rather than below, the waterline. The males of many of the mudskipper species unfurl their fancy top fins in a display to challenge other male rivals or to impress the females. They can also leap high into the air when they're trying to dazzle a potential mate. They are a very interesting fish, indeed.

The mudskipper in this book is a barred mudskipper. Look! He's showing off his fancy top fin for you. What do you think? Aren't you impressed?

Trout

The other main character in this book is a steelhead trout, which is a rainbow trout that has the special ability to live in fresh- and saltwater. All rainbow trout are born in freshwater, but steelhead trout head downstream to live in the ocean after they are born. The rainbow trout that stay and continue to live their lives in freshwater tend to be smaller and more colorful than the steelhead.

Steelhead trout swim back upstream to lay their eggs in freshwater, in a process called spawning. The female will find a fast-flowing stream, dig a hole called a "redd," and then lay up to 9,000 eggs at a time. The male fish then fertilizes the eggs and the female covers them up with pebbles from the streambed. After spawning, the steelhead trout return to the ocean.

Although the barred mudskipper and trout that travel through this book together wouldn't exist in the same habitat in the real world, they prove to be great friends in this one!